WILD EARTH SCIENCE

FLOODS

by Rachel Werner

a Capstone company — publishers for children

Raintree is an imprint of Capstone Global Library Limited, a company incorporated in England and Wales having its registered office at 264 Banbury Road, Oxford, OX2 7DY – Registered company number: 6695582

www.raintree.co.uk
myorders@raintree.co.uk

Hardback edition © Capstone Global Library Limited 2023
Paperback edition © Capstone Global Library Limited 2024
The moral rights of the proprietor have been asserted.

All rights reserved. No part of this publication may be reproduced in any form or by any means (including photocopying or storing it in any medium by electronic means and whether or not transiently or incidentally to some other use of this publication) without the written permission of the copyright owner, except in accordance with the provisions of the Copyright, Designs and Patents Act 1988 or under the terms of a licence issued by the Copyright Licensing Agency, 5th Floor, Shackleton House, 4 Battle Bridge Lane, London SE1 2HX (www.cla.co.uk). Applications for the copyright owner's written permission should be addressed to the publisher.

Edited by Ericka Smith
Designed by Tracy Davies
Original illustrations © Capstone Global Library Limited 2023
Picture research by Svetlana Zhurkin
Production by Katy LaVigne
Originated by Capstone Global Library Ltd

978 1 3982 4079 7 (hardback)
978 1 3982 4080 3 (paperback)

British Library Cataloguing in Publication Data
A full catalogue record for this book is available from the British Library.

Acknowledgements
We would like to thank the following for permission to reproduce photographs: Alamy: CPA Media Pte Ltd, 19; Associated Press: The Honolulu Advertiser/Bruce Asato, 17; Getty Images: MXW Stock, 26, Pavliha, 29, Warren Faidley, 6; Shutterstock: Aerial-motion, 15, AL Robinson, 9, Calin Tatu, 7, Carolyn Hutchins, 1, dynamic (map background), back cover and throughout, egd, cover, 3, Golden_Hind, 20, Hryhorii Patlakha, 23, Iain Frazer, 13, J.J. Gouin, 12, Jon Rehg, 28, lavizzara, 21, Lisa-S, 5, Michael Rolands, 25, pashabo, cover (logo), Steve Jett, 8, Viktor Gladkov, 4; USGS: 27, Paul Provencher, 11

Every effort has been made to contact copyright holders of material reproduced in this book. Any omissions will be rectified in subsequent printings if notice is given to the publisher.

All the internet addresses (URLs) given in this book were valid at the time of going to press. However, due to the dynamic nature of the internet, some addresses may have changed, or sites may have changed or ceased to exist since publication. While the author and publisher regret any inconvenience this may cause readers, no responsibility for any such changes can be accepted by either the author or the publisher.

Printed and bound in India.

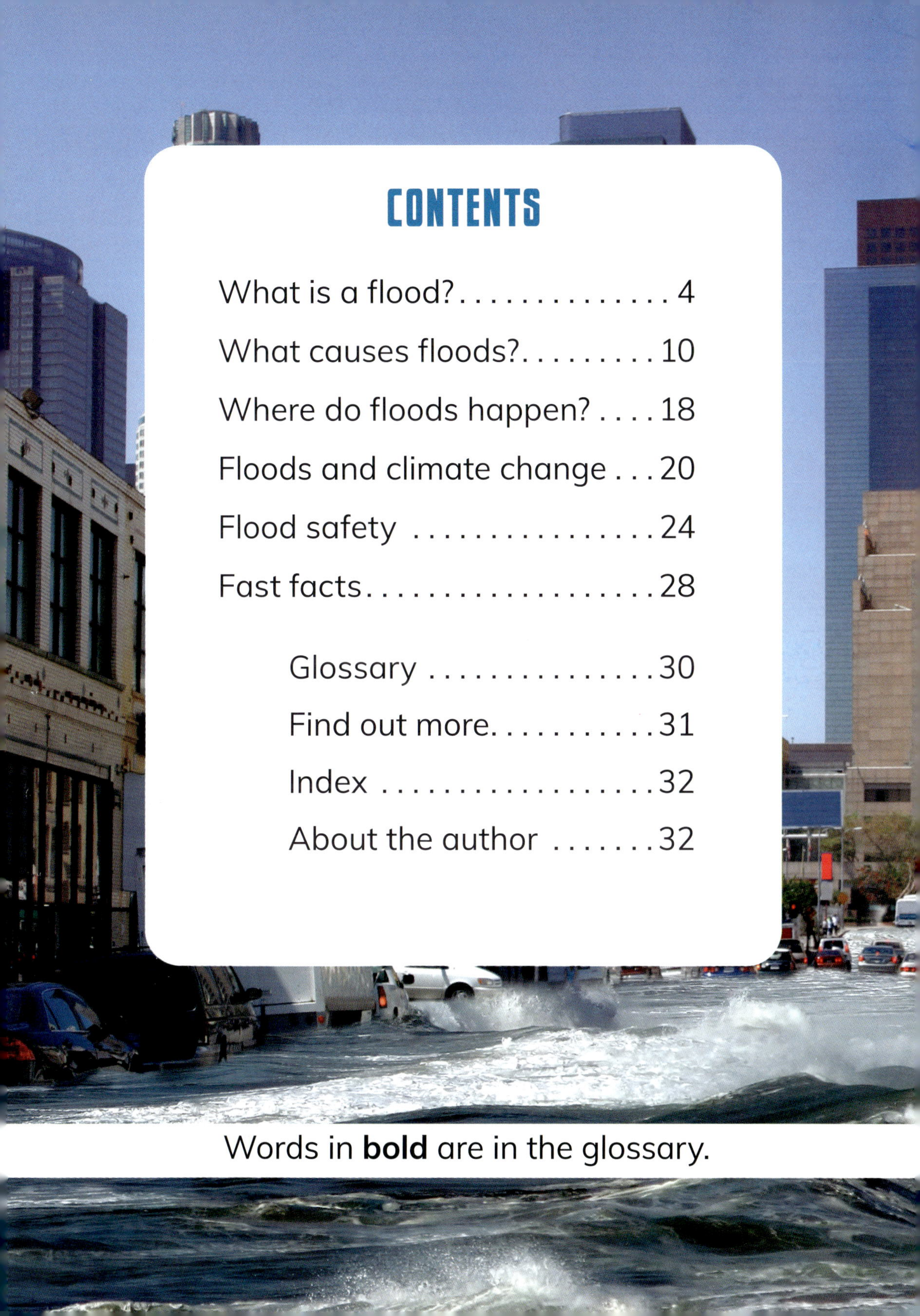

CONTENTS

What is a flood?............4

What causes floods?.........10

Where do floods happen?....18

Floods and climate change...20

Flood safety 24

Fast facts..................28

    Glossary 30

    Find out more..........31

    Index 32

    About the author 32

Words in **bold** are in the glossary.

WHAT IS A FLOOD?

Heavy rain falls. Rivers rise. The water has nowhere to go. It flows into the streets. It creeps into homes. It's a flood!

Flooded streets in Austria

Flooding happens when a body of water gets too full. It also happens where there's too much water in the ground. Flooding can happen over days. Or it can happen in a few hours. It may take weeks for the extra water to go away.

A coastal flood happens when high tides or waves pour water over low land. This is a **storm surge**. Weather events such as **hurricanes** and **tsunamis** can cause coastal floods.

Hurricane Irma hits Miami, Florida, USA, in 2017.

A flash flood in a Utah desert in the United States

A flash flood comes quickly. It can happen during a storm. It can happen when a lot of snow melts too fast. Sometimes it happens when a **dam** breaks.

Water from a river floods the land.

During a river flood, water swells over the banks of a river. It covers nearby areas.

During a flood, water may flow into floodplains. These are areas of flat land near bodies of water.

Urban floods happen when city storm drains do not work properly.

WHAT CAUSES FLOODS?

Extreme weather causes floods in many places. Some areas and some types of land are more likely to flood.

Dry land usually cannot soak up heavy rain. The hard soil cannot take in all the water. This causes flooding.

Places where snow and ice build up are also at risk. Ice can slow or block the **current** of a river. This is an **ice jam**. It can force water to overflow onto land.

An ice jam in the Redwater River in Montana, USA

Loss of plant life can also lead to flooding. Empty fields and soil **erosion** cause a loss of plants. When there are fewer plants, water can flow freely.

Erosion along the bank of a river

Loose soil near rivers and streams can wash away. The soil builds up in other places. This can change or block the current. These changes may lead to flooding.

Many dams are old. They can have leaks, cracks or breaks. Things such as earthquakes and climate change can weaken dams.

A dam that breaks is dangerous for nearby towns. People may not be ready for a sudden flow of water.

An old dam in Greece built in the 1920s

In 2006, the Kaloko Dam in Hawaii failed. After 40 days of rainfall, the dam broke. About 1.5 billion litres (400 million gallons) of water rushed into the nearby area. The flood swept 16 cars into the ocean. It killed seven people.

Water flows over a break in the Kaloko Dam.

WHERE DO FLOODS HAPPEN?

Floods happen all over the world. But some areas experience more floods than others.

The United States has a high number of floods. States such as California, Florida and Louisiana have many floods. They have coastal or urban areas where flash floods happen often.

Flooding in China in 1931

China had a huge flood in 1931. First, there was a two-year **drought**. Then, record amounts of snow and rain fell. Rivers overflowed. Some experts estimate the flood killed more than 3 million people.

FLOODS AND CLIMATE CHANGE

Warmer weather is causing more **precipitation** each year. Extreme heat creates more powerful storms.

A huge storm hit the Philippines in 2018.

Wind gusts are getting stronger. More water **vapour** forms as winds blow across warm ocean water. This can lead to hurricanes or other storms.

21

These storms hold more moisture because of the warmer temperature. That increases the amount of rain they produce. This can lead to flooding.

Hurricanes and other **tropical** storms are getting stronger. And they are causing more flooding around the world.

Flooding in Vietnam

FLOOD SAFETY

Walking or driving in a flooded area is not safe. The best thing to do when there are flood warnings is to leave. Get far away from the flooded area. Or find a higher place.

Remember that what seems like a small amount of water can do a lot of harm. Water that is moving quickly is more likely to be dangerous.

A floodway is a path that steers water away from some areas. Some floodways are natural. But people can make them too. Creating floodways is one way to prevent floods.

A marsh in Louisiana, USA

Another way is to add green spaces to help water drain. A **wetland** is a green space where soil can take in lots of water. Bogs, marshes and swamps are types of wetlands. They can help prevent floods. They soak up extra water like a sponge.

FAST FACTS

- 5.2 million properties in England are at risk of flooding.
- Just 0.3 to 0.6 metres (1 to 2 feet) of rapidly moving water during a flood can move a car.
- The deadliest floods ever happened in China in 1887, 1931 and 1938.
- Flooding can even happen in some of the hottest and driest places on Earth. The Sahara Desert flooded in 2003.

A flooded desert in Morocco

GLOSSARY

current movement of water in a river or an ocean

dam barrier built to block a body of water

drought long period of weather with little or no rainfall

erosion wearing away of land by water or wind

hurricane very large storm with high winds and rain; hurricanes form over warm ocean water

ice jam pieces of ice that clump together and block the flow of a river

precipitation water that falls from clouds to Earth's surface; it can be rain, hail, sleet or snow

storm surge sudden, strong rush of water that happens as a hurricane moves onto land

tropical having to do with a warm climate

tsunami large, destructive wave caused by an underwater earthquake or volcanic eruption

vapour gas made from something that is usually a liquid or solid at normal temperatures

wetland area of land covered by water and plants; marshes, swamps and bogs are wetlands

FIND OUT MORE

BOOKS

Climate Change (DKfindout!), DK (DK Children, 2020)

Earth (DKfindout!), DK (DK Children, 2017)

What are Floods? (Wicked Weather), Mari Schuh (Raintree, 2020)

Wide World of Weather: Weather and Climate Around the World (Weather and Climate), Emily Raij (Raintree, 2020)

WEBSITES

www.bbc.co.uk/bitesize/topics/z849q6f
Learn more about the natural world.

www.dkfindout.com/uk/earth
Find out more about Earth, from weather and climate to volcanic eruptions.

INDEX

California 18
China 19, 28
climate change 14, 20–22
coastal floods 6, 18

dams 7, 14, 16
droughts 19

earthquakes 14
England 28
erosion 12, 13

flash floods 7, 18
floodplains 9
floodways 26
Florida 6, 18

Hawaii 16
hurricanes 6, 21, 22

ice jams 10, 11

Kaloko Dam 16, 17

Louisiana 18, 27

river floods 8
rivers 4, 8, 10, 13, 19

Sahara Desert 28
storm drains 9

tropical storms 22
tsunamis 6

urban floods 9

wetlands 27

ABOUT THE AUTHOR

Rachel Werner is the founder of the Little Book Project WI. Her writing has been published by Off Menu Press, *Digging Through the Fat* and *Voyage YA*. A selection of Rachel's poetry is included in the anthology *Hope Is the Thing: Wisconsinites on Perseverance in a Pandemic.*